National Parks: The **Peak District**

Published in 2023 by:

Northern Eye Books Limited

Northern Eye Books, Tattenhall, Cheshire CH3 9PX
© Northern Eye Books Limited 2023

ISBN 978-1-908632-76-0

Text: Dennis Kelsall, Chiz Dakin

Series Editor: Tony Bowerman

Photographs: Dennis Kelsall, Chiz Dakin, James Grant Photograpy, Paul Newcombe Photography, AdobeStock, Shutterstock, Dreamstime

Design: Carl Rogers and Laura Hodgkinson

Dennis Kelsall and Chiz Dakin have asserted their rights under the Copyright, Designs and Patents Act, 1988 to be identified as the authors of this work. All rights reserved

A CIP catalogue record for this book is available from the British Library.

Printed in the UK on woodland-friendly FSC stock

Cover: The 'Salt Cellar',
Derwent Edge

www.northerneyebooks.co.uk

@northerneyebooks

@northerneyeboo

@northerneyebooks

For sales enquiries, please call 01928 723 744

tony@northerneyebooks.co.uk

Contents

MANCHESTER
Staley Bridge
Stockbridge
PEAK DISTRICT
NATIONAL PARK
Glossop
Derwent Resr.
STOCKPORT
A624
A57
Ladybower Resr.
SHEFFIELD
Marple
A57
10
8
6
Castleton
Hathersage
Whaley Bridge
A6
4
Chapel en-le-Frith
A623
R Derwent
MACCLESFIELD
A6
BUXTON
CHESTERFIELD
A537
A6
1
Bakewell
5
A54
2
7
A515
Congleton
A523
A53
MATLOCK
Hartington
R Dove
LEEK
9
R Manifold
3
A523
Carsington Resr.

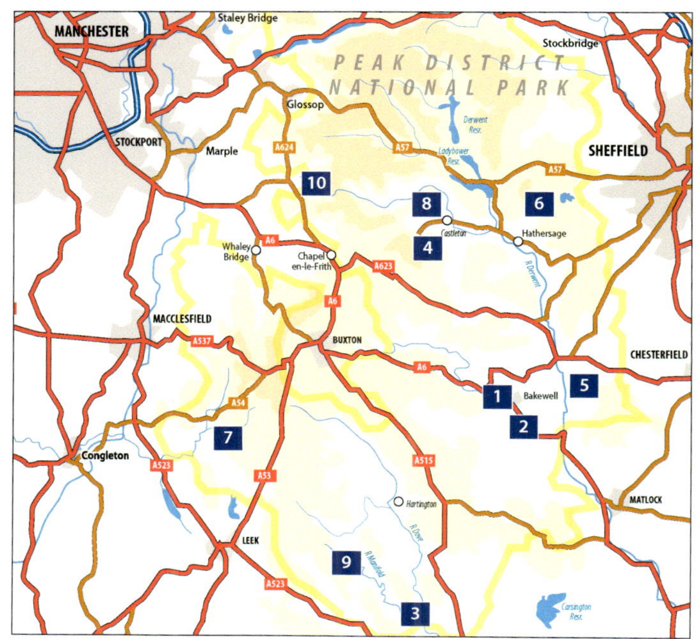

Britain's First **National Park**

CREATED IN 1951, THE PEAK DISTRICT NATIONAL PARK extends over six counties and is the second most visited of Britain's National Parks. Its highest point lies upon the seemingly remote Kinder plateau, where a mass trespass in 1932 marked the turning point in a long and sometimes bitter campaign that led to the creation of Britain's National Parks and the open access we enjoy today.

The high, peaty moorlands of the northern Dark Peak are founded on gritstone, their stark grandeur accentuated by impressive, weather-worn tors and edges. The moors extend out of the Pennines in two horns that enclose the limestone plateau of the White Peak, an upland pasture cleft by narrow gorges and dales. The transition between the two is abrupt and each has a distinctive character and beauty all its own: the wild openness of the north contrasting with the more intimate southern landscape, dotted with small villages and criss-crossed by old lanes.

The famous panorama of Monsal Dale and its viaduct from Monsal Head

The very best of the **Peak District**

These ten themed walks explore the contrasting faces of the Peaks — the gentle White and rugged Dark Peak.

Discover clear rivers and streams, ancient packhorse bridges and stepping stones. Walk through winding dales and valleys bright with wildflowers. Visit stately Chatsworth or marvel at the panorama from Monsal Head.

Tour upland reservoirs and dramatic rocky edges popular with climbers. Slog up Shutlingsloe or explore the open moorland and strangely eroded tors on Kinder Edge. Every one is a walk to remember.

"Indeed all Darbyshire is but a world of peaked hills, which from some of ye highest you discover ye rest like steeples or tops as thick as can be."

Celia Fiennes, *Through England on a Side Saddle*, 1697

TOP 10 **Walks:** The Peak District's best walks

HERE, PACKED INTO A SINGLE POCKET-SIZE BOOK, are the ten absolute best short circular walks in the Peak District National Park. They've been carefully selected — from the already hugely-popular themed *Top 10 Walks: Peak District* series — to showcase the finest and most enjoyable walks across Peakland. So, whether you fancy an easy stroll up a limestone dale, a stunning view, a pint in a country pub, a nice cup of tea and a scone, or something more challenging, there's plenty to go at here.

WALK WITH HISTORY
Chatsworth
page 28
ROCKS AND EDGES 
Stanage Edge
page 34
WALK WITH HISTORY
Lud's Church
page 40
WALKS TO A VIEWPOINT 
Lose Hill
page 46

MYSTERIOUS WALK
Thor's Cave
page 52

MOORS AND TORS
Kinder Edge
page 58

The Peacock, Bakewell

walk 1

The Peacock
Bakewell

What to expect:
Tracks, paths and a quiet lane; steep initial climb but more gentle descents

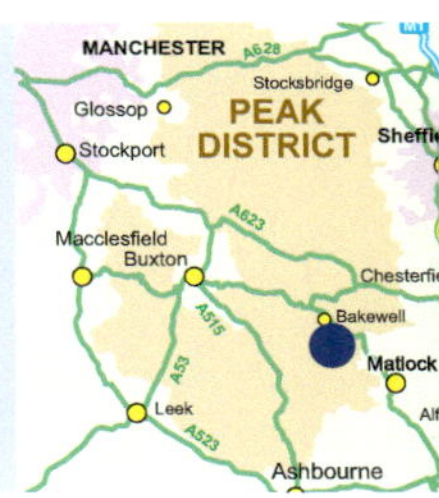

Distance/time: 11 kilometres / 6¾ miles. Allow 3 hours

Start: Smith's Island long stay pay and display car park, Bakewell

Grid ref: SK 220 684

Ordnance Survey Map: Explorer OL24 Peak District: White Peak area: *Buxton, Bakewell, Matlock & Dove Dale*

The Pub: The Peacock, Bridge Street, Bakewell, Derbyshire DE45 1DS | 01629 813635 | www.peacockbakewell.com

Walk outline: Leaving the town, there is a steep climb to Manners Wood, where the path levels for a fine stretch through the trees. Doubling back over the ridge, the next section dips above the head of Calton, crossing another wooded spur before falling across Chatsworth Park to Edensor. The return follows an old greenway back over the hill, descending steeply through woodland and past the old station to the town.

Famous for its tarts, Bakewell maintains its tradition as a thriving market town and has no shortage of coaching inns and hotels to serve hungry passers-by. One to try is The Peacock in Market Street, just across the river from the car park.

The Peacock, Bakewell

▶ The Peacock at a glance

Open: Every day
Brewery/company: Free house
Real ales: Local Peak Ales, guest Adnams, continental beers
Food: The menu presents a mix of traditional pub favourites and chef's specials, all freshly prepared to order
Accommodation: Twin, double and family rooms
Outside: Patio garden with tables for when the sun shines
Children & dogs: Well-behaved children and dogs are welcome

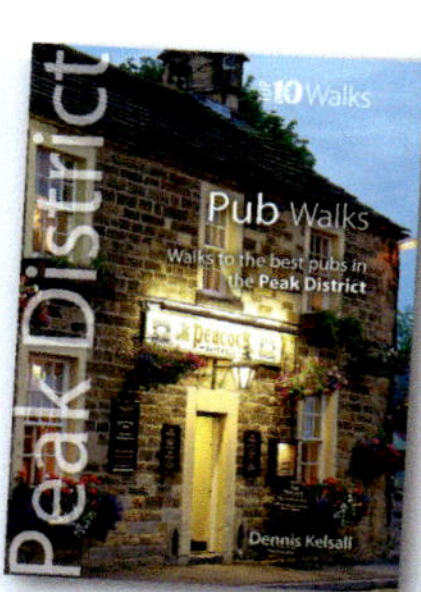

More pub walks ...

The Walk

1. Turning right from the car park, cross a bridge and immediately go left, signed 'Monsal Trail'. At **Coombs Road**, swing right, but leave left after 175 metres along a drive. Fork right through a kissing gate and climb by the right boundary to a gate in the top corner.

2. Over a bridge, continue up the hill. Where the bounding fences end, cautiously proceed forward across a golf course fairway and climb beyond into the trees.

3. At a fork, just beyond a stream, bear right on a concessionary path through **Manners Wood**. The gradient now relents and the way rises easily through long established woodland. The understorey is rich in wildflowers during early spring, exploiting the abundance of light before the leaf canopy develops. After levelling near the top of the hill, the way gently loses height, progressing through beech and other deciduous trees into a plantation dominated by conifers.

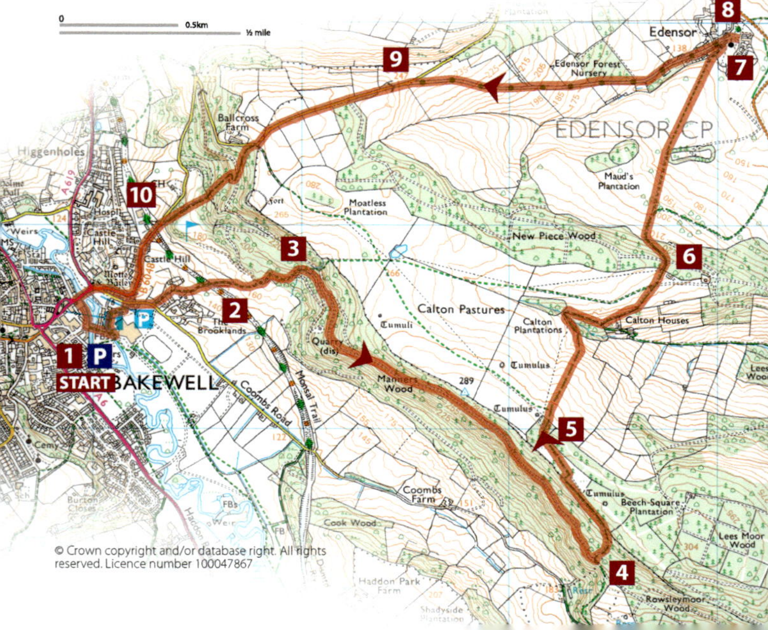

An unsurfaced lane lined with tall cow parsley, near Edensor

4. Reaching a junction, turn sharp left and head up the hill. The trail soon levels beside a stone wall running along the crest of the ridge. Keep going, shortly passing through a gateway and later curving away to descend to a stile at the edge of the wood.

5. Keep ahead past a waypost, following a green trod down the open hillside of **Calton Pastures**, the gradient steepening as it approaches the **Calton Plantations**. Pass through a gate and swing right beside the wall bounding the trees. Ignore a second gate lower down, staying with the now rising track. After 200 metres, the path moves away from the wall, climbing across the slope to a gate at the edge of **New Piece Wood**.

6. Follow a broad track between the trees. Emerging beyond onto the open parkland of the **Chatsworth estate**, head straight down the hill. Stay to the left of two successive stands of trees and then aim just left of the spire of **St Peter's Church** as it comes into view. Keep an eye open too for roe deer, which graze amongst the sheep.

Fragrant bluebells carpet the open glades in Manners Wood

7. Reaching the edge of the park, leave by a metal gate tucked near the corner, from which a stepped path winds down between cottages to come out in the village.

To the right is the church, designed by Sir Gilbert Scott, and an extensive graveyard in which lie the bodies of Sir Joseph Paxton, who was head gardener at Chatsworth and designed the Crystal Palace, and Kathleen Kennedy, President Kennedy's sister who married the 10th Duke of Devonshire's eldest son William.

You will also find the **Tea Cottage**, a great place to stop for afternoon tea.

8. Retrace your steps past the church but now continue along the rising lane through the village. At a junction where the tarmac ends, keep ahead with an old green lane, *its banks profuse in a variety of wildflowers such as stitchwort, bluebell, celandine, forget-me-nots and cow parsley. The increasing height opens views back across* **Chatsworth Park**.

9. Emerging onto a lane, head uphill. At a bend beyond the crest, bear left along an old, descending bridleway into trees. Lower down, cross a track and proceed cautiously over the golf course. Beyond another crossing track, emerge onto a lane and turn left.

10. Reaching the main road, turn left. Immediately over the bridge, double back left on a riverside path. After 75 metres, a path off right leads into **Market Square** beside **The Peacock**.

Otherwise, keep ahead to a footbridge, which crosses the **Wye** back to **Smith's Island car park**. ♦

Toxic beauty

Bluebells are a common woodland plant. They flower in April and May to form swathing carpets of delicate blue, their presence often indicating long-established or ancient woodland. When crushed, the bulbs produce a sticky substance that Tudors used for starching ruffs. It worked equally well as a glue; securing flights onto arrows for fletchers and was favoured by bookbinders: for, being toxic, it discouraged bookworm.

Hassop Station is now a popular café on the Monsal Trail near Bakewell

Hassop Station Café

An easy-going walk over rolling hillside paths and tracks following an old turnpike and former railway line

What to expect:
Grassy riverside path and meadow, gentle rolling hills, Monsal Trail, busy road crossing in Bakewell

Distance/Time: 5 kilometres/ 3 miles. Allow 2 hours

Start: Hassop Station, Bakewell DE45 1NW

Grid Ref: SK 222 689

Ordnance Survey Map: Explorer OL24 Peak District: White Peak area: *Buxton, Bakewell, Matlock & Dovedale*

After the Walk: Hassop Station Bookshop Café and Cycle Hire, Hassop Station DE45 1NW | 01629 815 668 | www.hassopstation.co.uk

Walk outline: From Bakewell's former railway station, a short stroll leads down to the riverbank, then along this to the old Newcastle Under Lyme to Hassop Hall Turnpike route. Rise on out of Bakewell on this over a couple of gentle hills to the Monsal Trail — a former rail line now converted to a multi-use easy going track. The café is just along the track, which then leads easily back to the parking at the top of Bakewell.

This former station turned café-bookshop and cycle hire centre offers an excellent cup of coffee, hot meals, with local wine or beer and a range of soft drinks. At the counter is a delicious display of cakes, but the sausage cobs are among the best in the Peak District.

Coffee and cake

▶ Hassop Station Café at a glance

Open: 09.00-17.00, 7 days a week (Additional late opening in summer)

Food and Specialities: Homemade cakes, toasties, soup to full meals. Breakfast baps, fresh local beef burgers and station platters. Gluten free and vegan options for cakes. Food is locally sourced where possible

Beverages: Fresh Barista-style coffee, range of teas and speciality teas, bottled soft drinks, bottled ale from Peak Ales and Thornbridge, wine

Outside: Picnic tables and sun terrace above the Monsal Trail. Large outdoor covered area. Wood-fired pizza oven for summer evenings

More tea shop walks ...

The Walk

1. From the **car park**, head down **Station Road** to a T-junction by the **Derwent River bridge**, on the edge of Bakewell. Cross the **A619** and take a lovely, easy-going cinder trail through a metal gate to **Scot's Garden**. This meanders next to the riverbank then cuts across a corner of meadow. Go through two gates as the river bends

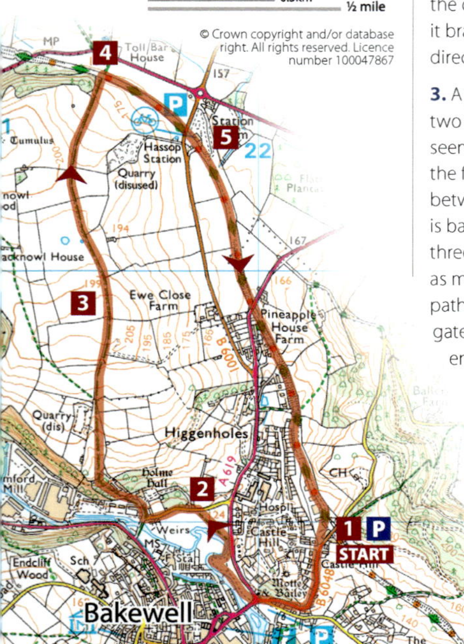

back to the path, then follow red-lined waymarkers across a small field to a residential lane.

2. Turn left onto this and follow it to the end of the public road (by **Riverside Business Park**). Turn right onto a gravel track, passing a blue plaqued house where Richard Arkwright Jnr once lived. The surface briefly roughens and steepens through **woodland**, then enters a grassy field. Rise up on the continuation vehicle track until it branches left, then maintain your direction to the top of the field.

3. A **green lane** now undulates over two low hills to **Hassop Station**. It seems to become greener as you top the first rise and begin a gentle descent between pasture fields. The second rise is barely perceptible; passage through three gates fairly close together is about as much indication as you get. The path narrows somewhat after the third gate, with summer undergrowth often encroaching.

This green lane was once the main turnpike, or toll road, between Newcastle-under-Lyme and Hassop Hall. Look out for an old cottage across the fields as it ends at the Monsal Trail — this was a Toll House during its turnpike days.

An undulating green lane winds between Bakewell and Hassop

4. Exit rightwards onto the **Monsal Trail** and follow this for about 400 metres along the former railway line to an **overbridge**.

5. Just beyond the bridge, turn left for the **café** at **Hassop Station**.

Once refreshed, it's now about 1.6 kilometres/1 mile along the **Monsal Trail** back to the start, passing under a road-bridge on the way. Go past a few industrial buildings on the right, and then turn right immediately before the **former station buildings** on a narrow cut-through to the car park to complete the walk. ◆

Stately stations?

The two stations of Bakewell and Hassop are a curious anomaly illustrating power and privilege. Although neither are central to the town, both could equally serve as its main station. Curiously, Bakewell station was built for the benefit of the Duke of Rutland and his Haddon Hall Estate (and bears his coat of arms in the walls); while Hassop station was built for the convenience of the Duke of Devonshire and his Chatsworth Estate.

The famous stepping stones at Dove Dale

Dovedale

A walk through the Peak's most famous dale from a picturesque Victorian estate village

What to expect:

Field and riverside paths; quiet lane; gentle climbs and one steep but short descent

Distance/time: 10.5 kilometres /6½ miles. Allow 3½ hours

Start: Ilam Hall, National Trust pay and display car park

Grid ref: SK 131 507

Ordnance Survey Map: Explorer OL24 *Peak District: White Peak area: Buxton, Bakewell, Matlock & Dovedale*

After the walk: National Trust Manifold tearoom, Ilam Hall, Ashbourne DE6 2AZ | 01335 350245 | www.nationaltrust.org.uk

Walk outline

The path from Ilam skirts the western flank of Bunster Hill, passing a crystal stream emanating from St Bertram's Well. After briefly following a quiet lane, the way crosses fields to the head of Hall Dale, a secluded, dry valley that leads to Dovedale. A riverside path winds through the gorge below towering rock formations. The final leg crosses grazing pastures behind the Izaak Walton Hotel back to the village.

Dovedale

Tourists have been flocking to Dovedale since the 18th century, awed by the soaring rock pillars and sheer cliffs lining the narrow gorge. The different features became endowed with Romantic names, some even acquiring an embellishing tale or two. At Lover's Leap, a maiden threw herself into the gorge in despair on hearing of her lover's death but, caught in a tree, she lived, to learn that he too was happily alive. Reynard was a local brigand and the cave his hideout, but tragedy struck when an inquisitive Victorian visitor was killed in attempting to ride his horse up the steep path.

Reynard's Cave

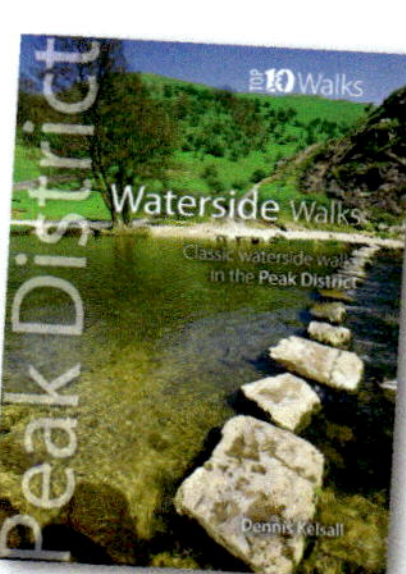

More waterside walks ...

The Walk

1. Walk back along the main drive of Ilam Hall and continue ahead through the village to the **memorial cross**.

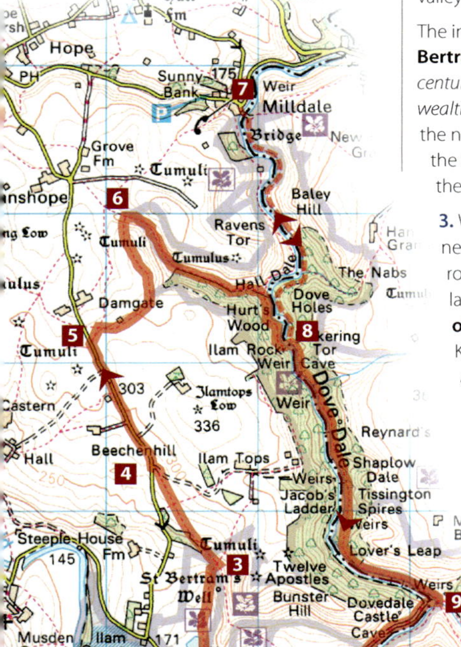

Fork left, but leave left after 200 metres through a small gate onto **Bunster Hill**.

2. Climb forward past the National Trust plaque to a signboard and carry on, picking up a field track towards Stanshope. Over a stile beside a gate, continue up the rising base of a shallow valley.

The intermittent stream is from **St Bertram's Well**; *named for an 8th-century Mercian prince who renounced his wealth and position to live as a hermit.* In the next pasture, make for a stile near the top right corner. Bear left above the wall, following it to a squeeze stile.

3. Walk forward to another crossing near the wall corner. Strike a diagonal route across the next large field, later passing above the hollow of an **old quarry** to a stile in the end wall. Keep the same line, crossing a track and then leaving over the lefthand wall onto **Ilam-moor Lane**.

4. Head up the hill. As the lane begins to fall, look for a stile immediately beyond a gate on the right.

A vast, water-eroded limestone arch guards Reynard's Cave

5. Diagonal paths criss-cross the field; look for a stile out at the top right corner near a derelict barn. Follow a track through gates passing the barn and then a **dewpond**. Beyond a gate at the very end, go left to a second gate.

Walking away, look back to see a lime kiln built into the hillside below a small quarry. The footpath stays beside the lefthand wall, but there are dramatic views into Hall Dale if you follow the fenceline over to the right instead. Fence and wall eventually meet at a stile.

Continue down a steep, grassy bank, which may be slippery in wet weather.

6. Over a stile at the bottom, turn right into **Hall Dale**. The path descends gently through the valley; the steep sides are initially bare, but farther on, become wooded on the right. Larch gives way to ash as the dale narrows, the accompanying wall thickly enveloped in moss. Rounding a corner, the **River Dove** can be heard and the path drops into the main valley. Turn downstream, shortly crossing a bridge below the lofty pinnacle of **Ilam Rock**.

Looking up Dovedale from just above the famous stepping stones

If you have time, there is a pretty 1.5 kilometre, or 1 mile, diversion upstream to Milldale (7) and **Viator's Bridge,** which is mentioned in Izaak Walton's classic 17th-century fishing treatise, *The Compleat Angler*. Return to this point to resume the walk downstream.

8. Continuing beside the river, the path resorts to a causeway as the gorge dramatically narrows. Where the dale later widens, look up left to see a splendid **natural arch**, behind which is **Reynard's Cave**. The path then climbs onto the rocky viewpoint of **Lover's Leap**, the stone steps full of fossilised crinoids, ancient sea creatures similar to the present-day sea lily. The path soon returns to the river, passing weirs containing shallow pools for trout.

9. As the main gorge swings right in front of **Lin Dale**, Victorian **stepping stones** cross the river. Alternatively, there is a bridge a little farther downstream.

10. Reaching the entrance to the **Dovedale car park**, bear right through a gate into the overflow car park, leaving right again in a few metres through trees to a stile.

Strike out behind the **Izaak Walton Hotel**, pausing to look back at the truncated pyramid of Thorpe Cloud. Over a couple of stiles, keep going across another large field. Beyond its far-left corner, **Ilam Hall** appears ahead, a developing track leading into a final pasture. Towards the end, drop left to the lane and go back through the village to complete the walk. ♦

Ilam memorial cross

The village cross at Ilam is a memorial erected by Jesse Watts-Russell to his wife Mary. Given the Ilam estate as a wedding present by his father, Jesse built the Gothic hall and laid out the model estate village. The memorial takes the form of an Eleanor Cross, of which twelve were commissioned by Edward I to mark resting-places on the route from Lincoln along which his wife's body was taken for interment at Westminster Abbey.

Winnats Pass and Mam Tor

Castleton & Cave Dale

An uncomplicated circuit combining the two dramatic gorges that cleave the limestone hills overlooking Castleton

What to expect:
Good paths and tracks, short road section. Steady ascent along Cave Dale

Distance/time: 7 kilometres /4½ miles. Allow 2¼ hours

Start: Castleton Visitor Centre beside the town's main pay and display car park

Grid ref: SK 149 829

Ordnance Survey Map: Explorer OL1 *The Peak District: Dark Peak area: Kinder Scout, Bleaklow, Black Hill & Ladybower Reservoir*

After the walk: Choice of pubs and cafés around the town

Walk outline

The walk leaves the town on a climbing path through Cave Dale, passing beneath the ruins of the town's ancient castle. Picking up old walled tracks, the way continues between upland fields to the head of Winnats Pass. Joining the lane, it heads down through the gorge to the Speedwell Cavern. The final leg gives fine views across to Mam Tor as it contours the hillside to the Peak Cavern, just above the town.

Castleton and its caves

Castleton sits below the edge of the Peakland limestone plateau looking across the Hope Valley to an impressive backdrop of Mam Tor and Lose Hill. The hills behind the town are honeycombed with caves and tunnels, some natural, but others dug over the centuries by miners in search of metal ore and minerals. Castleton is unique in Britain for having four show caves on its doorstep. The Peak Cavern, also known as the Devil's Arse, burrows beneath Peveril Castle and at one time housed a pub within its massive entrance. Speedwell, also passed on the walk, was worked as a lead mine, but has since flooded and can now be visited only by boat.

More dales and valleys walks ...

Mam Tor subsidence

The Walk

1. From the **Visitor Centre**, walk into town. At a bend, turn right past **St Edmund's Church**. Approaching the top, keep left past a green, once the site of the town's market, and bear left again into **Bargate**.

2. After 100 metres, branch right along a short, narrow street between cottages. Pass beneath rocky buttresses to a gate, from which a winding path begins a steady climb into **Cave Dale**. High above is the gaunt ruin of **Peveril Castle**, best seen in retrospect farther on. Progressing through a gate gap into the upper valley, the gradient eases as the gorge shallows towards its head.

3. At the top, beyond a couple of gates, the path diverges from the right-hand wall across the crest of the field. The impressive hill to the north is **Mam Tor**, the embanked defences of a prehistoric settlement clearly visible around its summit. Leave the far corner of the field through a couple of gates onto a walled track.

4. Turn right through a gate. Shortly reaching a fork in front of a second gate, take the right branch. Walk for 1.5km/1 mile, passing **Rowter Farm** and ultimately meeting a lane.

5. Go right to a junction and right again, the way signed to 'Castleton'. Initially there is no verge, but shortly, beyond a cattlegrid, the bounding walls end to open a grass swathe into the deepening gorge of **Winnats Pass**.

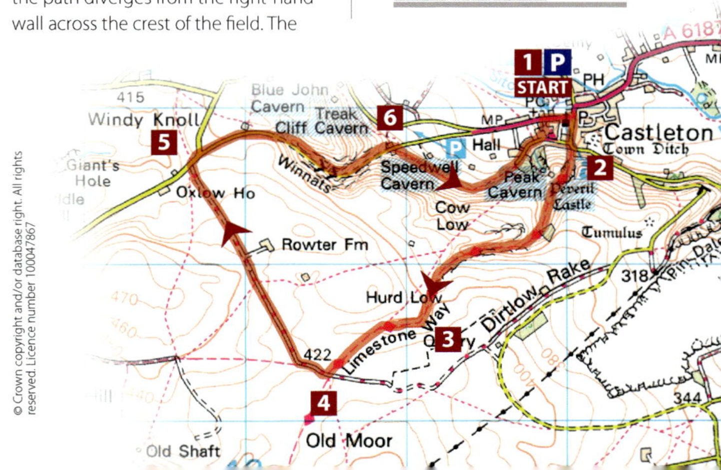

Cave Dale winds up through a limestone gorge below Peveril Castle

6. Beyond the entrance to the **Speedwell Cavern**, leave the lane through a gate on the right onto the National Trust's Long Cliff. A clear path leads along the edge of rough pasture. Ahead, the squat tower of **Peveril Castle** peeks through skyline trees while grassed heaps indicate lead mining across the hillside. Exit the fields through a gate below a wood and walk past cottages towards the town. A street to the right leads to the **Peak Cavern** at the base of a towering cliff, but the way back lies ahead. After crossing a bridge, go left beside the stream to meet the main road opposite the Visitor Centre, to complete the walk. ◆

Peveril Castle

Making the most of the natural defences afforded by the deep gorge of Cave Dale, this small castle was founded around 1085 by William Peveril, one of William's loyal supporters during the Norman invasion of England. The Peverils held extensive tracts of land in the Midlands, including Nottingham Castle, and the stronghold here was used as an administrative centre and hunting lodge for the royal Forest of High Peak.

Chatsworth House enjoys an idyllic setting

Chatsworth

Walk in the woods and parkland surrounding one of Britain's grandest stately homes

What to expect:

Woodland and field paths; a stepped climb may be slippery when wet

Distance/time: 6.5 kilometres / 4 miles. Allow 2-2½ hours

Start: Chatsworth House car park (fee)

Grid ref: SK 260 703

Ordnance Survey Map: Explorer OL24 *Peak District: White Peak area: Buxton, Bakewell, Matlock & Dove Dale*

After the walk: Edensor Tea Cottage (Chatsworth), Edensor, Bakewell DE45 1PH | 01246 582315 | www.edensorteacottage.co.uk

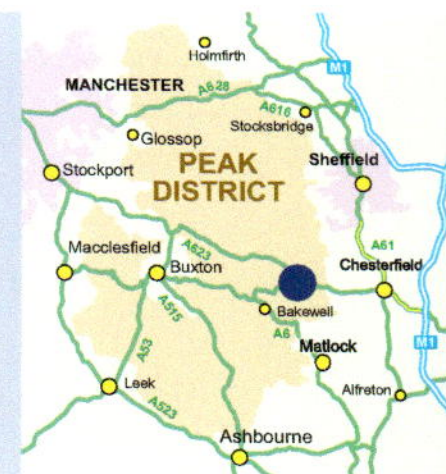

Walk outline

From the house, the walk climbs the wooded hillside to the 16th-century Hunting Tower. After visiting the lake, which supplies water to the grand fountain, it continues through the wood and along Dobb Edge. After dropping past Jubilee Rock, the route carries on across the deer park towards the River Derwent. The walk finally heads downstream to Queen Mary's Bower and Paine's Bridge, from there paralleling the main drive back to the house.

Hunting Tower

Chatsworth

Chatsworth has been home to the Cavendish family since 1549, when Sir William and his wife Bess of Hardwick bought the estate. After his death in 1553, Bess continued the work of building a grand house, although all that remains from her day is the Hunting Tower on the hill behind. The present hall has its origins in a rebuilding begun in 1687 by the 4th Earl (1st Duke) of Devonshire. It evolved into one of the finest stately mansions in the country and contains a wealth of fine furnishings and an impressive collection of art treasures.

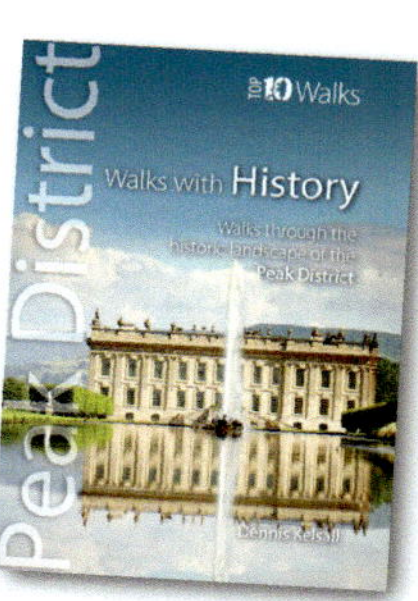

More walks with history ...

The Walk

1. From the top of the car park, take the drive signed 'Farmyard' and 'Playground'. Just before the farmyard entrance, slip through a gate onto the adjacent estate track and, directed by a sign 'Stand Wood Walks', continue up the hill. After 50 metres, rounding a bend, turn off onto a path on the left, which climbs through the trees to reach a higher track.

Cross to the ongoing path opposite, an occasionally muddy climb beside the gully of a stream that develops into a long flight of stone steps that may be slippery when wet. Emerging onto another track again, cross and go up beside the **Hunting Tower**, continuing along a short beech avenue to meet yet another track.

2. Turn right and then, at a fork, keep left, shortly reaching the tip of the **Emperor Lake**.

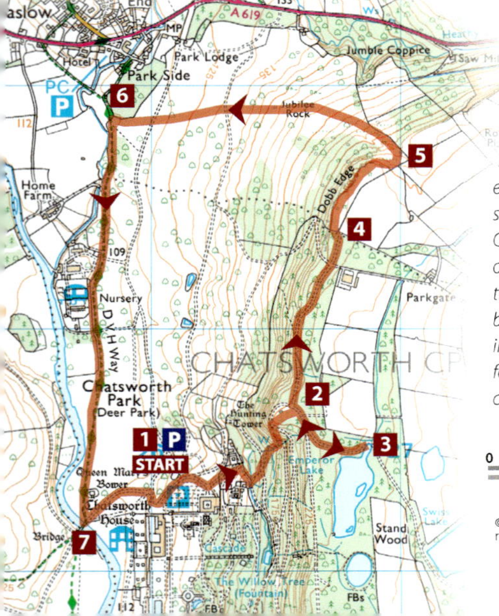

The Emperor Lake was created in 1843 to provide water for an immense fountain to celebrate a proposed visit by Tsar Nicholas I. Situated some 105 metres above the gardens, the eight-acre lake took just six months to complete, but in the event, the Tsar never arrived to see the magnificent spectacle. Capable of throwing a jet of water over 90 metres into the air, it was the highest fountain of its day and became the jewel of an already impressive water garden, created for the 1st Duke in the early 18th century.

The Emperor Fountain and the south front of Chatsworth House

Many features of that original garden have survived including the Cascade, a long flight of 24 steps down which water tumbles from the fountains of a 'water temple' presiding at its head, and the Canal Pond, a lake that extends south of the house for over 300 yards. There is also a fountain in the guise of a lifelike willow tree, which greatly impressed Celia Fiennes, a pioneering lady traveller who had no doubt seen it all in her journeys throughout the length and breadth of the country.

3. Walk back to (**2**), but this time, carry on a little farther to a cross-roads. Turn right, the way signed 'Robin Hood'. Walk on through a conifer plantation, keeping ahead where the track later turns into a **timber yard**. Just before reaching a gate at the end, swing off left, following the wall to a high stile.

4. Over the stile, the signed path sticks by the wall over to the right, but an informal path follows the rim of **Dobb Edge** to take advantage of the spectacular views. However, be careful for there are some long drops. *In places the edge has been quarried and towards the far end of the cliffs, the quarrymen*

Chatsworth House is one of the nation's favourite stately homes

have left a standing pillar beside which is an unfinished millstone.

As the edge runs out move back to the wall, where the path leads down to another high stile.

5. Instead of crossing, go left on a grassy swathe that descends with a shallow gully. Lower down, the path fragments, but keep heading forward at the edge of an open oak wood that has grown up amongst the boulders littering the apron below the edge. Aiming for a pair of wooden field gates that soon become visible, continue downhill, passing a large boulder known as the **Jubilee Rock**, carved in commemoration of Queen Victoria's Diamond Jubilee.

Cross a stile beside the double gates and, over the track, walk in the same direction across more parkland, now following a sign to 'Baslow'. Reaching a high deer fence, follow it left around the perimeter of a wood to meet a path entering the estate through the **Cannon Kissing Gate** from the village.

6. Turn left along the clear path at the edge of the park. There is a glimpse of the **River Derwent** tumbling over a weir as you shortly join an estate drive. Keep ahead at a junction by **White Lodge**, but after passing the cricket green you can move across to follow the water's edge. Approaching **Queen Mary's Bower**, return to the track and pass through a gate to reach the main drive by **Paine's Bridge**. Cross the drive and swing left on a path that leads through a gate back up to the house and car park to complete the walk. ♦

Paine's Bridge

The accession of the 4th Duke saw many changes to the park and gardens, sweeping aside the 1st Duke's baroque gardens for the more naturalistic style championed by 'Capability' Brown. The successful Palladian architect James Paine, already working on new stables for the house, was commissioned to design a bridge across the river, which he sited to take best advantage of the view to the house.

An abandoned millstone below Stanage Edge

Stanage Edge

A pleasant wander along the most popular edge in the Peak District

What to expect:

paths are uneven in Whitfield Gill, one lengthy ascent

Distance/time: 8 kilometres / 5 miles. Allow 2½ hours

Start/finish: Upper Burbage Bridge car park, beside A625

Grid ref: SK 259 829

Ordnance Survey Map: Explorer OL1 The Peak District: Dark Peak area: *Kinder Scout, Bleaklow, Black Hill & Ladybower Reservoir*

After the walk: The Norfolk Arms, Ringinglow Road, Ringinglow S11 7TS | 0114 230 2197 | www.norfolkarms.com

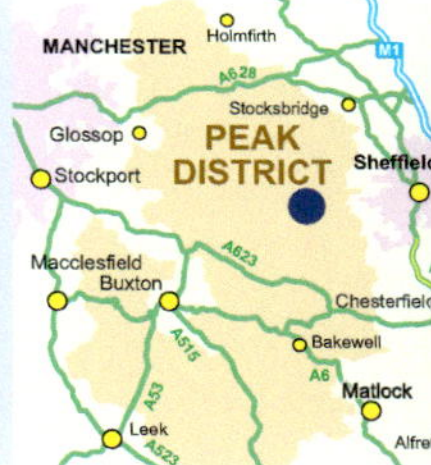

Walk outline

Striking across the moss, the route bypasses the Cowper Stone to gain the eastern end of Stanage Edge. An easy path traces the rim of the escarpment, passing above a rocky aerie known locally as Robin Hood's Cave. Farther on, an old packhorse track offers a detour to Stanedge Pole on its low hill in the middle of the moor. Returning to the edge, the way drops back through Stanage Plantation and on across the hillside footing the cliffs. The final leg climbs back onto the edge and reverses the outward path to the car park at Upper Burbage Bridge.

Gritstone climber

Stanage Edge

Running for some 5.5 kilometres/3½ miles, Stanage is the longest of the Peak's eastern gritstone edges and defines an abrupt boundary to the Hallam Moors on the outskirts of Sheffield. Once part of a private grouse shoot, it was forbidden land to walkers and climbers, who nevertheless braved the gamekeepers for the stolen pleasures of its rocky challenges and superlative views. Today the area is designated 'open access' and is justifiably popular.

More rocks and edges walks ...

The Walk

1. From the car park, follow the lane west from the bridge, leaving ahead on the bend along a broad path across the moss. Approaching the escarpment, the prominent detached rock seen over to the right is the **Cowper Stone**, which, despite its size, offers several difficult challenges to rock climbers. Picking an easy passage between the rocks, the path rises onto the escarpment and leads past a 'trig' column perched upon a cantilevered slab of rock.

There is a fine view along the length of the edge, while equally eye-catching in the other direction is the vista beyond Hathersage along the Derwent Valley. Looking west of north across the unbroken expanse of White Path Moss, keen eyes will spot Stanedge Pole, while a glimpse to the foot of the cliff below the 'trig' will reveal a group of abandoned millstones. These can be conveniently visited on the way back.

2. Carry on along the rim of the edge. After 800 metres/½ mile watch for a path branching left through a shallow gully (SK 244 835), which leads to a narrow terrace fronting **Robin Hood's Cave**.

Agile explorers will be able to scramble through the cave to emerge onto a

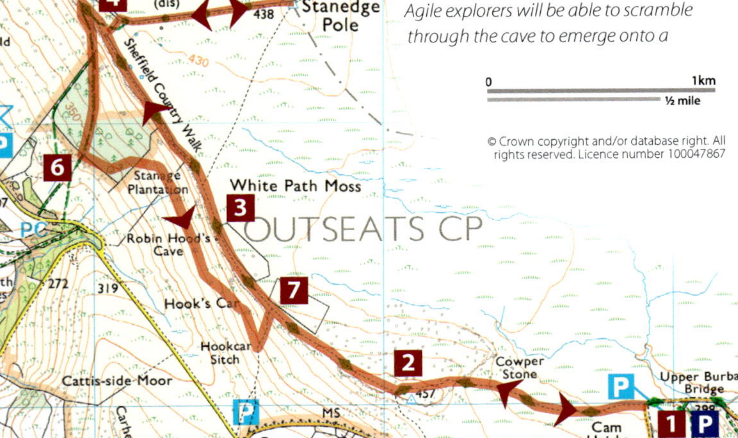

0 — 1km
— ½ mile

Alternate sunlight and short showers enliven Stanage Edge

balcony that gives a superb view across the valley, but take care near the edge as there is a precipitous drop.

3. Having taken in the view, climb back to the top path and continue along the edge, shortly joining a broken wall above a dramatic section of cliff. Walk on some 800 metres/½ mile, crossing a ranch stile to reach a junction of paths.

4. Go right to a broad track, the **Long Causey** and follow it right for 400 metres/¼ mile to the **Stanedge Pole**.

The tall wooden post is a medieval guide

stoop, which stands on the watershed of the moss from which there is a view down to the Redmires Reservoirs, the Rivelin Valley and Sheffield.

5. Retrace your steps to the top of the cliffs and follow the path right for 100 metres. At a fork, branch left, the path almost immediately doubling back to descend below the line of cliffs towards the top corner of the **Stanage Plantation**. Through a gate, follow the path into the trees. Cross a sparkling **spring** dashing from the rocks above and continue between the rowan, alder,

Panoramic views from Stanage Edge towards Millstone Edge

birch and oak to emerge through a gate at the bottom.

6. Ignore the obvious onward path dropping towards the lane and instead go left on a faint trod rising beside the fence. It shortly joins a broader path that leads to a gap in a wall on the right. Breaking from the trees, carry on across the hillside, where the expanse of deep bracken is broken in summer by occasional tall spikes of foxglove. Criss-crossing sheep tracks and climbers' paths can be confusing, but keep generally ahead with the more obvious path, contouring the slope, remaining parallel to the line of cliffs above.

Eventually, the path forks prominently beside a **large boulde**r in which a basin has been hollowed from its top. Take the right branch, which angles down towards a roadside car park by a junction. However, shortly reaching another obvious junction of paths, turn left and climb towards the cliffs. The path winds easily between the boulders onto the top of the edge.

7. Turn right towards the **OS 'trig' point**, which lies about 500 metres away. As you approach the 'trig', look for a path branching down between the rocks to the base of the cliffs. *There you will find the group of millstones seen earlier in the* *day. They were abandoned when white bread became fashionable and the market collapsed in the mid-18th century.*

Return to the top of the cliffs and retrace your outward track past the 'trig' point and back to the car park at **Upper Burbage Bridge** to complete the walk. ♦

Stanedge Pole

The track to Stanedge Pole follows the course of a Roman road that linked the forts at Templeborough and Navio. The same route was subsequently followed by packhorse teams and known as the Long Causey, the tall pole being erected as a conspicuous marker on this otherwise featureless landscape. Although the wooden pole is periodically renewed, dates carved on its rocky base stretch back to 1550.

The deep natural cleft of Lud's Church

Lud's Church

An intriguing forest gorge, once used as a secret meeting place by 14th-century religious dissidents

What to expect:
Generally clear forest and moorland paths

Distance/time: 10.5km/ 6½ miles. Allow 3½ hours

Start: Gradbach car park, on the narrow lane to Gradbach Mill

Grid ref: SJ 998 662

Ordnance Survey Map: Explorer OL24 *Peak District: White Peak area: Buxton, Bakewell, Matlock & Dove Dale*

After the walk: The Ship Inn, Barlow HIll, Wincle SK11 0QE | 01260 227217 | www.theshipinnwincle.co.uk

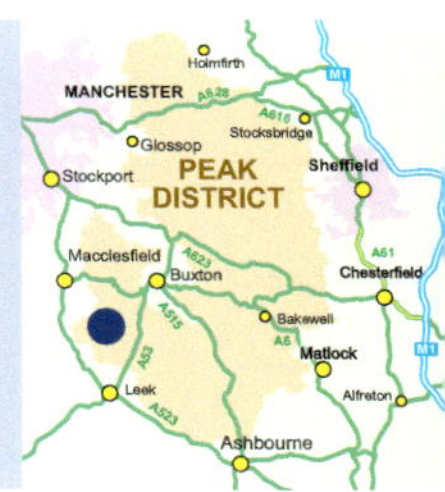

Walk outline

From a riverside car park, the walk follows the Dane Valley past a former silk mill to Danebridge, where a nearby pub offers an inviting lunch stop. The return climbs onto the moor past a striking rock outcrop, the Hanging Stone, then drops into the trees to find the secluded defile of Lud's Church. The way continues through Forest Wood before finally descending along the steep flank of Black Brook's valley.

Lud's Church

A natural chasm formed by a landslip along the line of a geological fault, Lud's Church has always been a place of mystery. Sheer 15 metre-high walls thick with dripping moss and ferns contain a narrow passage some 100 metres long and, supposedly only on mid-summer's day does the sun shine full into the cleft. Pagans reputedly used it for solstice ceremonies, while Walter de Lud-Auk, a 14th-century follower of the religious dissident John Wycliffe, held secret services here, out of sight of the Catholic Church. Some say, too, that the place is the Green Chapel of Arthurian legend, where Sir Gawain encountered the Green Knight.

Clear signposts

More walks with history ...

The Walk

1. From the car park, follow the lane right, shortly bearing off to **Gradbach Mill**. Wind right and then left past the mill and café onto a riverside path. Continue at the edge of a field and then along a track. Reaching a sharp bend, cross a stone stile on the right and drop to a narrow footbridge spanning **Black Brook**.

2. Turn right past its confluence with the **River Dane**, bearing left onto a path contouring the woodland edge. Rising to a fork, keep right and carry on above the river.

3. Eventually, after crossing a stile, the path leaves the trees to cross a sloping meadow. Over another stile a fenced path runs between paddocks to **Back Forest Farm**. Crossing its drive, the ongoing path continues towards a second farm at **Back Dane**, which soon comes into view.

4. Meeting a track, fork right, but as it then swings to the buildings, keep ahead on a grass trod. The path meanders through a larch wood, in time dropping over a stile into a meadow. Bear left towards the river, picking up a track at the far end that rises to a lane

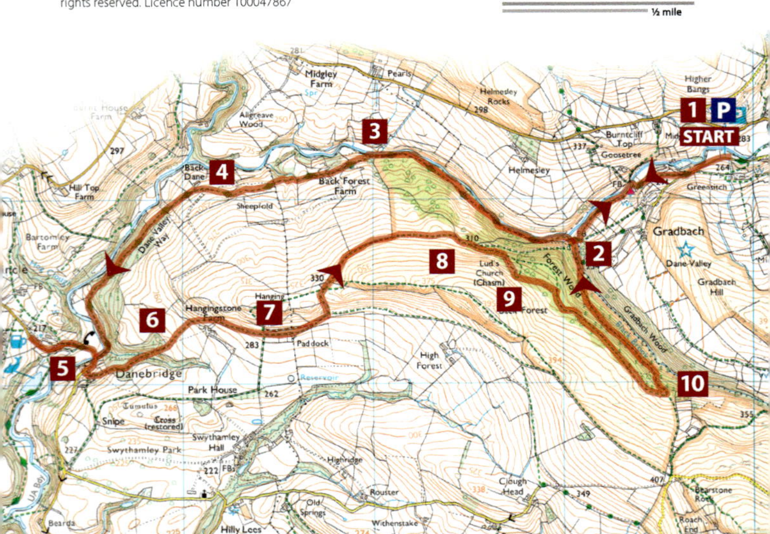

At its upper end, the mossy cleft of Lud's Church splits in two

beside **Dane Bridge**. Cross the bridge to visit the **Wincle Beer Company's brew house** (first track off on the left) and **The Ship Inn**, a short distance farther up the hill.

5. Return across the bridge and head up the lane, leaving after 100 metres along a path on the left signed to 'Back Forest' and 'Gradbach'. Crossing a drive, walk on between hedges and then at the bottom of a small field to enter a wood. Meeting another path, go right, climbing through a narrowing valley.

6. Emerging into open pasture, strike out to a wall stile just left of the far trees. Go right towards **Hangingstone Farm**, but immediately branch left on a rising path to a second stile. Signed right towards 'The Roaches', a track runs below the stark, fist-shaped outcrop of the **Hanging Stone**.

7. Reaching a junction, bear left of ahead along a concessionary path signed to 'Gradbach'. At the end, turn left in the direction of 'Lud's Church' along a moorland track. Keep on over the crest, the way gently descending beyond towards the fringe of **Forest Wood**.

Shutlingsloe dominates the horizon from the hill above Lud's Church

Entering the trees, continue to a fork by an eye-catching outcrop.

8. Keep with the path ahead, but after 200 metres, beside a wooden rail, watch for a cleft in the rock wall bordering the path. Turn in and drop left into the ravine of **Lud's Church**.

Green with age, the dark, secret chasm of Lud's Church is the ideal setting for legend and tales of mystery infused with the supernatural and when tendrils of mist veil the trees above, you will swear that you are not alone. Despite being far from Sherwood Forest, the ravine was one of the haunts of Robin Hood's band of outlaws.

More sinisterly, it is said that a huntsman thrown by his horse from the lip above forever roams the forest shrouded in the moss and dead leaves on which he died, seeking revenge on lone travellers.

Walk through the deep gully, taking the right branch towards the far end, where more rugged steps climb out to the top.

9. Follow the path forward amongst the trees, shortly reaching a crossing path. Go right, towards 'The Roaches', the way wandering on through the forest. Ignore a path later signed off onto the ridge and carry on until you reach a T-junction.

10. 'Gradbach and Danebridge' are

indicated to the left. Bearing left at a later fork, continue across the steep valley side high above **Black Brook**. Eventually the path falls to meet the stream at a ford. Remaining on this bank, carry on a little farther to a footbridge.

Cross and retrace your outward steps past the **Gradbach Mill** to the car park to complete the walk. ♦

Gradbach Mill

The original 17th-century flax mill was rebuilt following a fire in 1785 and adapted to spin silk for what was then a growing local industry. But remoteness and the development of steam power rendered it uneconomic and, by 1875, the business had gone. The building later housed a sawmill and joinery shop before being converted into a youth hostel in 1984. It is now an outdoor education centre.

Back Tor and Lose Hill on the Great Ridge

Lose Hill

Was this once Wessex's hill in a battle against Northumbria of the 7th Century? They had good views if so!

What to expect:

Steep slopes, country lanes, ridgeline path, short but steep rocky holloway

Distance/time: 9 kilometres/ 6 miles. Allow 3½ hours

Start: Village Car Park, Hope

Grid ref: SK 171 835

Ordnance Survey Map: Explorer OL1 The Peak District: Dark Peak area: *Kinder Scout, Bleaklow, Black Hill & Ladybower Reservoir*

After the Walk: Grasshopper café, Castleton Road, Hope S33 6RD | 07976 067338 | www.facebook.com/hoppercafehope/

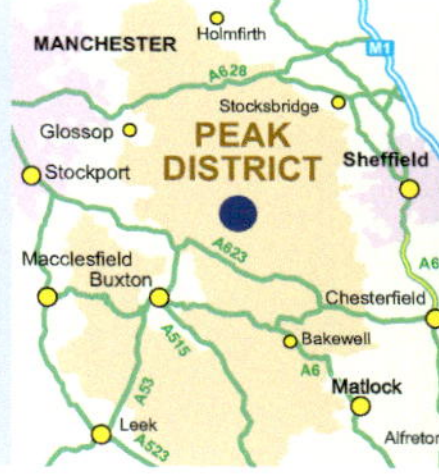

Walk outline

A hidden footpath leads out past a mix of small fields and residential housing to larger pastures. It's roughly a straight but steep line up to Lose Hill's Crimea Farm. The now broader path curves up to the summit, where there's a fantastic 360 degree panorama plus a view along the ridge to Backtor Nook. The descent to Hollowford Lane is rougher underfoot, but makes a quick descent into Castleton. And finally there's a lovely valley path beside a stream, through fields, back to Hope.

Lose Hill toposcope

The Great Ridge

Lose Hill is at the easternmost end of the Great Ridge between Edale and the Hope Valley. Along with its neighbour Win Hill, it was the site of a long-forgotten battle between Saxon Wessex and Angle Northumbria. The Wessex army, camped on Lose Hill, was significantly larger, and when they sensed victory they pushed forward into the valley between the two hills. Only to be massacred by boulders rolled from Win Hill by the wily Northumbrians. How true is the tale? No-one knows, but it makes a great story and exists in written form back to the 1800s.

More walks to viewpoints ...

The Walk

1. Opposite the **village car park**, take a footpath just right of the **Grasshopper Café**. This leads up steps, past a small meadow and through a snicket to a residential road. Follow this to a T-junction and cross the larger road.

2. From here it's roughly 1.5 kilometres towards **Lose Hill**: virtually straight ahead all the way to a **prominent barn** on the hillside. On the way, you'll pass through a succession of paths through small fields, cross a sagging **suspension bridge** over a little-used **railway line** and pass a small

stables soon after the bridge. There's also a paralleling short track at one point; the footpath keeps to the right. As you get further from the village, the fields get larger, and the hill steeper.

3. Cross a small **boardwalk bridge** shortly below the **barn**. Shortly above the barn, the path takes a left across the hillside and above a **house**, before veering right and uphill again. As the final summit approaches, fork right and over a couple of stiles to enter **access land**, then rise up a steep **stone pitched path** to **Lose Hill summit**.

There are fantastic 360 degree views from the top. From right to left there's a great view of Win Hill, Ladybower Reservoir and

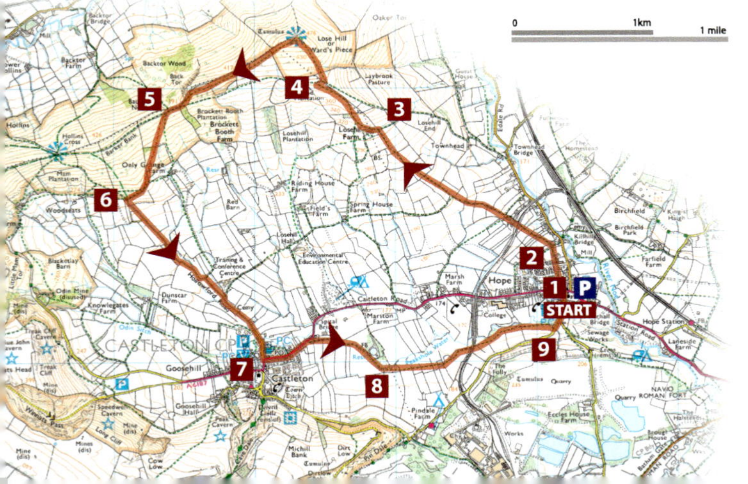

The distinctive rock cairn at Back Tor Nook on the Great Ridge above Castleton

Derwent Edge, out across the Noe (Edale) Valley to the Kinder plateau and along the 'Great Ridge' to Back Tor, Hollins Cross and Mam Tor. The view down into the Hope Valley isn't bad either.

4. Enjoy the panorama at the summit, then head left along the **ridgeline** towards Mam Tor, leaving access land at a stile. At the top of **Back Tor** an impressive **cairn** marks the start of a short but steep descent on the ridge.

5. Cross the wall by a stile, then immediately fork left twice in quick succession to head diagonally down a long grassy path (concessionary bridleway). It may be boggy just before you pass a couple of small stands of **woodland**, then bend right above a wall line. The path braids a little here; if you head high to avoid a muddy section you'll likely have a steeper rocky descent down to the wall line.

6. Turn left at a **five-ways crossing of paths** and down an often damp **rocky holloway**. Emerge onto the top of a lane, descend this to a junction, then turn right and continue the descent

The undulating, grassy ridge looking towards Lose Hill

to a T-junction with the main road in **Castleton**.

7. Turn left and pass **The Peak Hotel**. Near a bend left in the road, take a stony lane (public footpath) rightwards towards Hope. This ends at a **stream**; turn right here and go through a gate into sheep pasture. There's now a lovely waterside path for about 500 metres to a sharp bend left in the stream. Veer right here to a stile in the far right corner of the field.

8. You now cross several small grassy fields, then take care across an unexpected **railway line** — a continuation of the one you crossed earlier on the suspension bridge. Despite appearances this is still in use: it leads to the Hope Cement Works. Cross another field, then follow a wire fence line marking the field boundary with the **stream valley** back to a country lane, with one brief, but obvious, shortcut across a longer loop of stream.

9. Turn left down the lane, passing a **pinfold** just before you re-enter **Hope**.

The rules on the pinfold here date from 1947 but pinfolds were a common method of dealing with stray animals in Medieval times. Often a stick was carved with a notch to represent each animal. After being split, one half went to the landowner, and the other to the 'pinder', or pinfold-keeper. Once the strays' owner had paid the landowner, he was given their half-stick. This was taken to the pinder and 'tallied', or matched, with the other half and the animals released.

Turn left onto the main **village road** to complete the walk. ♦

'Ward's Piece'

The other accepted name for the summit of Lose Hill — Ward's Piece — comes from the purchase of the summit area by the Sheffield and District Federation of the Ramblers in 1945. They dedicated it to their founder (a dedicated, lifelong advocate of rambling) GHB Ward before handing it over to the National Trust to preserve for everyone to enjoy. This was one of the earliest forms of access land.

Two figures emphasise the sheer size of Thor's Cave

Thor's Cave

Two dramatic caves overlooking the capricious River Manifold

walk 9

What to expect:
Dramatic cave visit with a steep descent, rocky spots and a longish climb

Distance/time: 6.5 kilometres/4 miles. Allow 2–3 hours

Start: Wetton car park, Carr Lane, Wetton DE6 2AF. Overflow parking is sometimes provided in a nearby farmer's field

Grid Ref: SK 109 551

Ordnance Survey map: OL24 The Peak District *(White Peak Area)*

After the Walk: The Royal Oak, Wetton DE6 2AF | www.royaloakwetton.co.uk | 01335310287

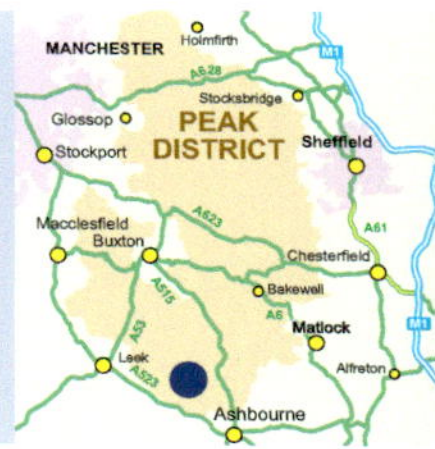

Walk outline

A straightforward track leads from Wetton to Thor's Cave. A steep descent via steps and stony ground leads through woodland to a footbridge over the Manifold (usually dry here). There follows an easy stage along an old railway line, to the café at Wetton Mill, where a second cave can be visited. The return is via a typical dry Derbyshire dale and a long, gradual ascent through sheep pastures back to Wetton village.

Thor's Cave and Nan Tor

The huge oval entrance of Thor's Cave overlooks the Manifold valley. Daylight pouring through its two openings mean that the vaulted interior can be explored without artificial lights, though care is needed on the polished limestone.

The quieter Nan Tor Cave, just off the footpath behind the Wetton Mill tearoom, is sometimes cited as an alternative to Lud's Church (see Walk 6) as the location of the 'Green Church', the scene of Sir Gawain and the Green Knight's legendary meeting described in an anonymous medieval poem.

Entrance to Thor's Cave

More mysterious walks ...

The Walk

1. From the **Wetton car park**, turn right past a stone barn in the field on the left, and then right again into a walled lane signposted to 'Wetton Mill'. Pass between two farms, then turn left at the next junction. After 50 metres, take a signposted concessionary track on the left. After 600 metres, beyond a gate and stile, turn right by a 'Wetton' fingerpost into the field on your right.

2. Bear left down the field, passing a wall corner and continue on an obvious, well-worn path across the hillside towards the cave. After a hand-gate, bear right (not towards the top of the hill) onto a path that curves under the cliff to the entrance to **Thor's Cave**.

3. Having explored the cave, take the stepped path in front of the main entrance that winds down through

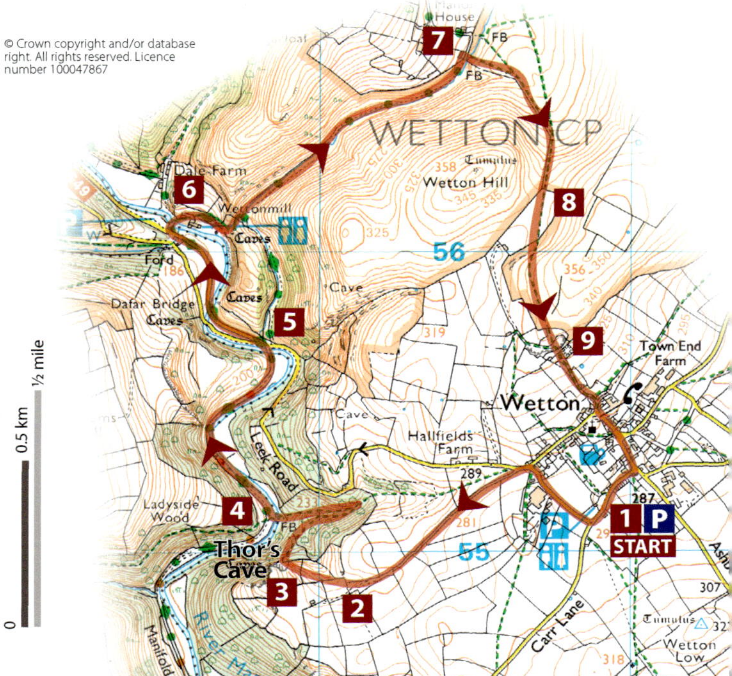

Nan Tor Cave is reached by a path above Wetton Mill

the wood. In the interests of erosion control, ignore any short-cuts on the left until you reach a major crossing path at the bottom of the side-valley, where you turn left (downhill). Follow the path down to the **footbridge** over the (normally dry) **River Manifold** and join the **Manifold Way**, a surfaced cycle and footpath, beyond.

The River Manifold passes under the old packhorse bridge at Wetton Mill as a sparkling limestone stream, but normally disappears into its limestone bed a short distance downstream. The dry riverbed runs below Thor's Cave and the waters only reappear near Ilam, several miles downstream.

4. Turn right and follow the Manifold Way along the valley bottom for half a mile until you cross the river again and meet a public road.

5. Turn left and take the right-hand fork, with a 'Weak Bridge' sign. Cross the dry riverbed once more and continue to the junction at **Wetton Mill**. Turn right over the **old bridge** and bear right to walk in front of the **café**.

The Manifold Valley seen through the main entrance and 'West Window'

6. Follow a signposted footpath between the **farmhouse** (left) and **former stables** (right) up to a gate and into a field. To visit **Nan Tor Cave**, turn immediately left, returning the same way.

Nan Tor Cave is sometimes suggested as an alternative setting for the Green Church, where Sir Gawain confronted the Green Knight. Although Lud's Church is the better-known candidate, in some ways Nan Tor, with its tree-hung interior open to the sky, seems to fit the description in the medieval account rather better.

Continuing along the public footpath, climb the rocky path through a shrubby area, then bear left when it opens out and descend via a hand-gate to the bottom of the unnamed dale. Turn left and follow the path up the dale bottom until you pass a **small swallet** on the right and reach a gate into a metalled road.

7. In front of the **farmhouse**, turn right through a tight **squeeze stile** and cross the stream via a **clapper bridge**. Follow the footpath up the slope and then follow the wall on your right as it climbs through sheep pastures between two hills.

8. Towards the top, cross a stile in the fence (ignoring a wall stile on your right) and leave the wall to follow a path across the field to another stile. The rocky path beyond climbs then levels off across the grassy hillside to a gate and **squeeze stile**, before descending through an **old quarry** to a farm track.

9. Follow the track ahead down into **Wetton village**; bear left past the **Manor House** and pass the **Royal Oak** on your right. At the next road junction, turn right (signposted to Grindon) back to the car park to complete the walk. ◆

Limestone lair

Thor's Cave holds little mystery for 'proper' cavers, having no significant passages beyond the enormous entrance chamber, but has fascinated visitors for centuries, and attracts rock climbers. Nineteenth and early 20th-century excavations found evidence of human occupation since the Stone Age, including at least seven human burials. The dramatic cave featured in Ken Russell's 1988 horror film The Lair of the White Worm, *starring a youthful Hugh Grant.*

Looking into Edale from Swine's Back

Onto the edge of **Kinder**

A strenuous walk from the valley onto the rim of the Kinder plateau with grand views

What to expect:
Long, steady climb on field and rugged moorland paths, returning along a good track

Distance/time: 10.5 kilometres / 6½ miles. Allow 3½ hours

Start: Bowden Bridge pay and display car park

Grid ref: SK 048 869

Ordnance Survey Map: Explorer OL1 *The Peak District: Dark Peak area: Kinder Scout, Bleaklow, Black Hill & Ladybower Reservoir*

After the Walk: The Sportsman Inn, Kinder Road, Hayfield SK22 2LE | 01663 741565 | www.thesportsmaninn.co.uk

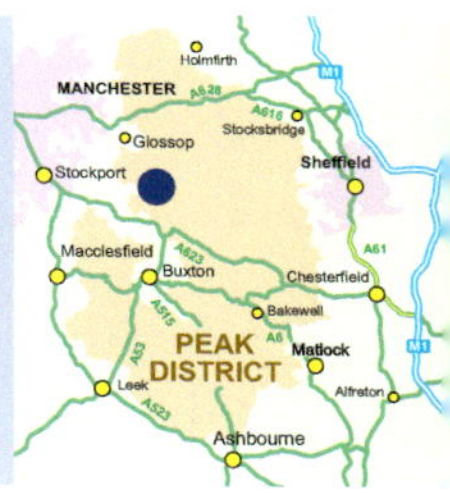

Walk outline

After following a lane and track to Tunstead Clough Farm, the way takes to the fields to reach the foot of Kinderlow End. A clear moorland path then rises across Kinder Low's steep flank, eventually broaching the edge beside the Red Brook gully. With the hard work over, it is an enjoyable ramble over Kinder Low and down to Edale Cross, from where a packhorse track leads back into the valley.

Kinder

Kinder Scout will forever be remembered by ramblers for a mass trespass in 1932. Some 500 members of Manchester and Sheffield walking clubs rallied on the hill to protest the injustice of being denied lawful access to England's open country. Although neither the first nor the last, the size of the gathering and the harshness of punishment meted out made the trespass a turning point in the campaign and eventually led to the enactment of The National Parks and Access to the Countryside Act in 1949. The Peak District National Park was the first to be created in 1951, and a plaque was later placed in the Bowden Bridge car park to commemorate the Trespass.

Barn below Kinder

More moors and tors walks ...

The Walk

1. Take the lane opposite the car park entrance, which crosses the **River Sett** and then swings left in front of the **Hayfield Camping and Caravanning Club site**. The lane bends again at the river's confluence with the **Kinder**, which is spanned by an old packhorse bridge, known locally as the **Roman Bridge**. Carry on beside the Sett to the next bridge. Cross, but just before a second bridge, leave ahead through a gate along a metalled track to 'Kinderstones and Tunstead House'.

2. After a sharp right-hand bend and bridge, bear right at a fork, the track winding past a cottage and **Tunstead House** to a gate and stile. Walk forward at the field edge and then bear slightly right across the next field. Keep climbing across successive fields towards the prominent bluff of Kinderlow End, eventually passing through a couple of gates onto the open moor. Go left to a final gate and stile at the foot of **Kinderlow End**.

Stone field barns, remote from the main farm became a feature of hillside pastures during the 18th century, assisting farmers to overwinter herds of cattle. Hay harvested during the summer was stored in an upper loft, the stalls below providing shelter from the elements for the animals.

3. Keep straight ahead, a clear path developing that gently climbs across

© Crown copyright and database rights 2016. Ordnance Survey. Licence number 100022856

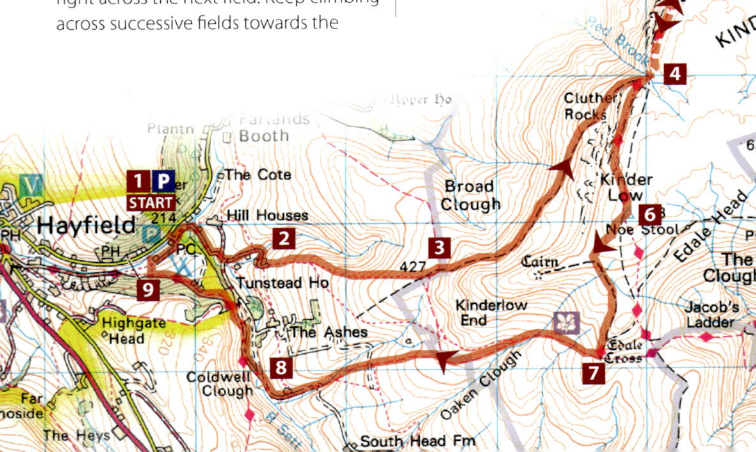

The setting sun illuminates Kinder's famous gritstone edge

the flank of the hill. Beyond a stream gully, the path becomes more rugged, wandering between the scattered boulders of **Cluther Rocks** for another 800 metres/½ mile. Approaching the gully of **Red Brook** (SK 078 879), watch for the path bearing off to the right to emerge onto the top of the edge beside the head of Red Brook. Should you miss it, the onward path soon narrows and turns in to meet the stream lower down the gully. Although there is an easy scramble out on the far bank, the best course is to retrace your steps to find the proper path.

(The top of the **Kinder Downfall [5]** lies some 800 metres/½ mile north along the path to the left and is worth a detour if you have time to spare.)

4. Otherwise turn right, shortly reaching a cairn. (To the left a rough trod picks across the moss towards Point 636, the highest point of **Kinder Scout**. Although it lies only 800 metres/½ mile away, the terrain is demanding and the detour is inadvisable in poor weather or for those without excellent navigation skills.)

The main path continues ahead past more cairns, shortly levelling to reveal

A curtain of rain closes on the eastern the edge of Kinder Scout

the **Kinder Low 'trig' column** perched upon a large boulder over to the left.

6. From the trig, head south of west to regain the main path beside a large cairn. Follow it away, gently losing height to a fork by another cairn. Take the left branch, which soon becomes flagged and leads to a second fork. Again keep left, the way gradually descending towards the hillock of **Swine's Back**. The path passes it on the right to join a wall, following that down to emerge through a gate onto a broad track at **Edale Cross**.

7. Follow the track right through a gate, just beyond which you will see the cross, tucked away in a small alcove to the right. An old packhorse route, the track leads off the hill, later becoming metalled and eventually reaching a junction. Keep ahead, passing a farm and shortly arriving at a fork.

8. Pass through the lefthand gate, marked 'Horses and Cycles', crossing a stream to follow a rising track above a beech wood. Carry on to the crest of the hill, where the **Pennine Bridleway** joins from the left. A few metres farther along, bear left onto a rough track signed to 'Hayfield'. The way soon levels, running to a gate at the edge of a wood. Immediately beyond, take the right fork

and descend at the edge of the trees.
Ignore a stile beside **Stones House** and
continue down to a crossing footpath
from Elle Bank.

9. Follow it over a stile on the right,
dropping to a **campsite**. Through

consecutive gates, cross its drive and
then turn right on a riverside path that
leads up to **Bowden Bridge** beside the
car park to complete the walk. ◆

Edale Cross

*Thought to have been erected originally by Cistercian
monks from Basingwerk Abbey in the 12th century,
Edale Cross marks the junction of the old parish wards of
Glossop, Hopedale and Longdendale. Discovered fallen
and buried in the peat, it was re-erected in 1810 by five
forward-thinking local farmers, whose carved initials it
now bears.*

Useful Information

Visit Peak District & Derbyshire
The Peak's official tourism website covers everything from accommodation and special events to attractions and adventure. **www.visitpeakdistrict.com**

Peak District National Park
The Peak District National Park website also has information on things to see and do, plus a host of practical details to help you plan your visit. **www.peakdistrict.org**

Visitor Centres
The main Visitor Centres provide free information on everything from accommodation and transport to what's on and walking advice.

Bakewell	01629 816558	bakewell@peakdistrict.gov.uk
Castleton	01629 816572	castleton@peakdistrict.gov.uk
Moorland Centre,		
Edale	01433 670207	edale@peakdistrict.gov.uk
Upper Derwent	01433 650953	derwentinfo@peakdistrict.gov.uk
Marsden	01484 222555	marsden.visitorinformation@kirklees.gov.u

Rail Travel
Four railway services cross the National Park:

The Hope Valley line

The Derwent Valley line

The Manchester to Buxton line

The Manchester to Glossop line

Information is available from National Rail Enquiries on 08457 484950 or **www.nationalrail.co.uk**

Bus Travel
Peakland's towns and many of the villages are served by bus. Information is available from Traveline on 0871 200 22 33 or **www.traveline.info**

Weather
Online weather forecasts for the Peak District are available from the Met Office at **www.metoffice.gov.uk/outdoor/mountainsafety** and the Mountain Weather Information Service at **www.mwis.org.uk**